Best Business Practices for Landscapers

WISDOM FROM LEADERS IN THE GREEN INDUSTRY

PAUL JAMISON

Best Business Practices For Landscapers

Paul Jamison

Copyright © 2021 Paul Jamison

ISBN: 978-0-578-97701-0

www.GreenIndustryPodcast.com

Dedication

I would like to dedicate this book to Bryan Race and Beverly Mayer.
You guys have been my friends throughout the years. Throughout
the mountain tops and valleys, I appreciate your steadfastness and
faithfulness to encourage me to pursue God's will.

I am grateful for your friendship.

Thank you.

Contents

Preview

Michael Crabtree says, "Revenue is for show, profit is for dough." In this book, I want to share time-tested business best practices that lead to a healthier bottom line and lasting success. In my previous book, *Cut That Grass and Make That Cash,* I shared about my journey including the many mistakes I made in my first decade as a landscaping business owner and what I learned from the missteps. In this book, however, I wanted to dive into the nitty-gritty of how businesses that have lasting success have achieved their successes. I will share the winning principles, habits, traits, and techniques that I have discovered having interviewed hundreds of business leaders and executives.

As host of the Green Industry Podcast, I have had a unique opportunity to get to pick the brains of some very intellectual, thoughtful, and successful business people. These conversations are shared in the over 500+ episodes of the Green Industry Podcast. It would take weeks to binge-listen through all that content and so in this book I wanted to provide a concise summary of those "key takeaways." There are many similar traits, attributes, techniques, and methods that proven winning businesses are employing and I can't wait to share them with you.

What are they doing right? What are their reasons for success? How have they achieved their victorious accomplishments? How are these businesses built to last?

1

Become An
Overnight Success

Caleb Auman hosts the Kid Contractor Podcast. He also runs a million-dollar landscape business near Columbus, Ohio in beautiful Fairfield County, Ohio. Caleb's business journey is super motivating as he persevered through some extremely difficult times to eventually come out on the other side triumphant. His business today is quite profitable and Caleb is finding a "sweet spot" in balancing his business operations with also making sure his marriage is thriving and his children are being raised in a healthy environment. The Auman's actually host an annual event called *Together In The Trades* that is a summit for couples in business. The main emphasis is how to achieve success in both your business and in your marriage and family.

The first ten years in Caleb's business were disastrous. Caleb, like so many go-getters, tried to outearn his stupidity, but eventually, his sloppy business management caught up with him. He was all over the place in so many ways and what finally knocked Caleb to his knees in desperation prayer was when the IRS chased him down for failing to file taxes for several years.

Caleb thoroughly enjoyed the construction aspect of his landscaping business. He finds great satisfaction in building stone patio pavers, retaining walls, and beautiful outdoor spaces. But, the mediocre effort on the business side of things is where Caleb got himself in trouble. Thankfully, two people stepped in and helped save Caleb's business. One of these lifesavers was Caleb's accountant Woody Winfree who helped him get on payment plans with the state of Ohio and the IRS to clean up the back taxes. The second hero is Brittany Nicole. She was friends with Caleb and they eventually fell in love. She graciously and mercifully accepted all of Caleb's flaws and back taxes and decided to team up with Caleb both in marriage and business. Brittany is now the owner of the company and over the last decade, Auman Landscape

LLC has had a mighty transformation.

In episode #73 of the Green Industry Podcast, Caleb and Brittany share the in-depth story of how they met, fell in love, got married, and over several years dramatically turned their business around. Here is an abbreviated summary of their stirring story. First, they had to address their massive pile of debt. They started their clean-up efforts by implementing what financial author Dave Ramsey calls a "scorched earth" policy--stripping their lifestyle to bare necessities. Caleb credits a Dave Ramsey book he read during that time as giving him the blueprint of how to pay off his debts. The Auman's made big sacrifices to their lifestyle to live on as little as possible and they worked their "butts off" to increase income. Brittany helped Caleb get more organized and systematized in his business. With many other adjustments and pivots, they were executing their new business plan, and although Auman Landscape LLC was not off life support it was beginning to be profitable. Eventually, the Columbus Dispatch recognized them as a Top 5 Landscape Company in the Columbus, Ohio area. Their story is impressive and so is the Kid Contractor Podcast.

One of Caleb's go-to lines on his podcast is that he is an overnight success twenty years in the making. Yes, Caleb does have a profitable business that grosses over a million dollars annually. Yes, Caleb does have a large and respectable Instagram following. And he is successful and I suppose those who gander through his highlight reel on Instagram may think Caleb makes it look easy. But, the reality is Caleb is not an overnight success. He has been in business for over twenty years and has learned many difficult lessons through the school of experience. One principle that he hammers home time and time again on his show (which I am an avid listener of) is that persistence and consistency are crucial. Once you determine the right things to implement in your business, it is then essential to do those things over and over again. This takes grit and endurance, but it's what really works.

Three companies, that I have interviewed on location for my podcast, that have really impressed me are Kohler, The Toro Company, and ECHO. Kohler has been in business since 1873 and their engines division has been operating since 1920. The Toro Company started in 1914. And ECHO is the baby in this conversation as they have been in business since 1972. Now I like engines, lawnmowers, and power equipment ...so I was a nerd when I had the opportunity to tour these companies' manufacturing facilities. What impressed me beyond the efficient assembly lines and grand buildings was their consistency and tenacity throughout the decades. These are not "flash in the pan" companies. They have been around for a long time and have achieved great success.

In this book, there will be no gimmicks or get-rich-quick schemes. But, I will share time-tested principles that have worked throughout the ages. We will explore the blueprint to profitability and true lasting success. So let's dive into why so many businesses like The Toro Company, ECHO Power Equipment, Kohler Engines, and smaller businesses like Auman Landscape LLC are winning. What is their recipe for success? Keep reading and take notes.

Reflection Question:

What would you change if you could about your business?

2

Exceeding
Expectations

The phrase KISS, Keep It Simple Stupid is thought to have been coined by Kelly Johnson. In business, this is a good reminder, keep it simple! At the end of the day, a key component is making sure our customers are satisfied. I have interviewed hundreds of thriving business leaders and one common denominator is their focus on making sure the customer is genuinely happy with their product or service. Many of the great companies take it a step further. Satisfaction is not good enough. They want clients who are elated with them.

While on a Podcast Tour up and down the East Coast I became hungry near Columbia, SC, and pulled off the highway to stop for lunch. Exploring my options, I noticed the line at Chick-fil-a was wrapped around the building not once, not twice, but an astounding three times! This fascinated me.

My next appointment was not until two o'clock that afternoon and it was only around noon. With plenty of time to spare before my next podcast recording and experiencing a sudden craving for some hot Chick-fil-a waffle fries, I pulled into the parking lot.

A pro tip I learned from listening to Clark Howard on the radio was to park and go inside and order. This is faster than waiting through the drive-thru line. And so, I squeezed into one of the only available parking spaces and then walked inside to the aroma of hot and juicy chicken.

With my first stop, even before ordering, being the restroom I took note that the bathrooms were clean. As someone who travels a lot, I always pay attention to what restaurants, gas stations, and hotels are clean. A raggedy unclean bathroom is irritating to me. Thankfully, this particular Chick-fil-a, as most of their franchises do, kept their bathroom nice and clean.

Now in line to place my order, it was pleasant to know the wait time would be short. All cash registers were in use and it looked like they had beefed up staff, and it would be just a minute before I was placing my order. That gave me just enough time to contemplate if I was going to get grilled chicken or go for the spicy chicken sandwich and hot waffle fries. I placed my order, a spicy chicken sandwich, no tomato, large waffle fry, and a bottle of water. Shortly after that they called me by my first name and delivered my hot lunch. Then, I took a seat at a clean table and enjoyed the delicious meal.

Dining a lot at Chick-fil-a over the years, I had high expectations for this experience. I can honestly say the folks at Chick-fil-a exceeded my expectations as a customer that day. But, later on in the trip, while staying at a popular hotel chain, I had quite the opposite experience. Let me share that story then I will tie this altogether of why it is imperative to make sure our customers are satisfied.

After another long day on the road, during the same tour, I stopped off in Midlothian, Virginia to stay the night at a hotel. I was exhausted from all the traveling throughout the tour and the next day I was scheduled to do ten podcast interviews. You read that correctly, ten podcast interviews scheduled for one day. Needless to say, I had high expectations that I could quickly check into a hotel, unpack, shower, and get a good night's rest. After a long day and what had been a tiring week, my energy levels were sinking and I was hoping that if I got some good sleep and a hot breakfast I would be rejuvenated, refreshed, and ready to crush it the next day.

My hotel selection was based on location. It was next to a mall very close to where Naylor Taliaferro, who was hosting me the next day, lived. He recommended the area and since it was a brand name hotel I figured it would get the job done. When I arrived, I noticed a lacrosse team in the lobby with their parents. Perhaps that was a red flag I should have not ignored, but regardless I waited in line at the front desk and eventually checked in. My day started in Columbia, South Carolina and the drive was torturous as a tropical storm was moving through on my way to an interview in Raleigh, North Carolina. After the podcast recording, I continued to drive through the heavy winds and rain to finally arrive at this hotel in Midlothian, Virginia. Physically tired plus mentally and emotionally depleted described my current state as I'm waiting to check-in.

As I entered the hotel room I noticed it was filthy. Above the toilet was a mound of dust on the shelf that held the towel. I recognized many other areas that could have been cleaned better. However, dead tired, I put my suitcases down, hopped in bed, hoping to fall asleep, and wake up the next morning feeling like superman.

I am somewhat something of a light sleeper. At home, my bedroom is very quiet. And in addition to the peace and quiet, I also have a noise machine that gently plays the sweet sounds of the waves of the ocean colliding into the sand at the shoreline. Most nights while at home I sleep like a baby, waking up refreshed and ready to take on the day. As I lie in the hotel bed I couldn't help but notice the foul odor coming through the air conditioner. The AC had been cranked up to get the room nice and cold, but to my surprise, it also spread a nasty smell. It smelled like body odor and was horrible. At home, I rely on my favorite candle to create a pleasant smell, but what I was breathing in was quite the opposite. Finally, I was able to close my eyes after a wild day of driving through heavy rain and winds for over nine hours. And that is when the doors started slamming. The lacrosse team was staying on my floor. I am assuming they were high schoolers because they were staying in a big group with their parents. The parents were probably attempting to go to sleep while the high schoolers were coming and going from their hotel rooms. The problem was each time these doors would shut they would make a loud noise. I could not compute how many times this happened throughout the evening. Why don't these kids smoothly shut the door? How many times could they possibly go in and come out of these rooms? This was so frustrating. I was too tired to change rooms to another part of the hotel and just wanted to fall asleep as I just lie in this nasty-smelling room discouraged that it was so loud.

Eventually, falling asleep way past my regular bedtime, I woke up bright and early in the morning when someone down the hall slammed the door first thing in the morning before the sun had even come out. They probably did not intentionally slam it, but the way these strong hotel doors close creates a loud noise. No need for my alarm clock to go off. This was definitely my worst night of sleep in a long time.

I thought this would be a good time for a hot shower, maybe that would energize me since I got very little sleep. Walking to the sink to put my contacts in I noticed a huge hair in the sink. It looked like it was a foot long. Much longer than my hair and there was another hair on the knob to the faucet. This was disgusting. Heading into the bathroom to get a shower and grabbing a towel I noticed two dark black gnarly hairs from a previous guest on the towel that was supposedly clean. Ah, hell no (ghetto voice)! You have got to be kidding me. This was the only bath towel left. The previous night I put the other towel at the crack of the door to try to block out the light coming into the room through the hallway. I like to sleep in the dark and cold. Long story short or short story long, this hotel stay was a disaster. My goal of a good night's sleep and being rejuvenated did not happen.

After very little sleep, finding manscaped hairs on the towels, faucet, and sink I went down to grab some breakfast. Could they possibly mess up some hot fresh bacon and eggs? Well, when I got to the breakfast station they had "grab n go". Well, I passed on the imitation Apple Jacks and the not so Golden Grahams and grabbed my car keys to go to First Watch down the street.

The reality is this hotel did not meet my expectations. Not even close. The hotel stay was an underwhelming experience and I will never ever stay at that raggedy hotel again. Honestly, likely I will never stay at that brand's properties again. I had an expectation of a clean room, a reasonably quiet hotel, and a hot breakfast. And they were zero for three in my expectations.

In summary, my Chick-fil-a experience was pleasant and I will likely return to Chick-fil-a often. My hotel stay was unpleasant and I will NOT return as a customer to that specific hotel and will think long and hard before staying at any of their other properties. As business leaders, I know we can be so hyper-focused on our profit and loss statements, on stewarding our relationships with employees and subcontractors and so many other important business dealings. Often I have noticed we can so quickly lose focus on our customers. What kind of experience are they having with our services and products? Are they happy, satisfied raving fans? Or are they somewhat satisfied with our average service/product? Or even worse, are they disappointed like I was at the hotel?

I am learning that the best practice is to make sure our customers are happy throughout their entire experience with our companies. My married friends tell me "Happy Wife, Happy Life." Well in business "Happy Customer, Happy Business Owner". Of course, there is more to it than that. We need to achieve profitability and so on. But at the end of the day, as business leaders, we need to be reminded of who is paying the bills around here. It is our customers. What are their thoughts, experiences, and feelings? It is good to frequently press "reset" and really evaluate how we are taking care of our customers. Making whatever necessary adjustments along the way to ensure they are more than satisfied is crucial. My goal is to exceed customers' expectations every single time. In this book, many of the strategies, tips, and best practices I share will tie back into how we can add massive value to our customers and truly exceed our customers' expectations. Keep it simple, keep the customers pleased.

Reflection Question:

How can you add more value to your customers?

3

It Is Not What You Know
It Is Who You Know

"A good name is rather to be chosen than great riches, and loving favor rather than silver and gold." - Proverbs 22:1.

We have established that it's important to maintain a good reputation with our customers. It's also valuable that we have a good reputation overall. You never know who is watching and what possible networking opportunity is right around the corner. One of my mentors, Otha Turnbough, encourages folks to live "squeaky clean." There are many benefits of doing the right thing. People who are dependable, honest, and trustworthy are rare in today's world. But, they are out there, and connecting with the right people can produce huge results.

When I was a little kid my father would take me to the house of his friend Wilbur. Wilbur lived next to a golf course and had a lake in his backyard. He was a big shot businessman and I remember him telling me, "It's not what you know it is who you know." At the time I did not fully compute this saying. However, after being in business a number of years, interacting with and even interviewing for the podcast some highly intelligent people, the more I appreciate Wilbur's memorable comment and have seen it in action.

One of the most memorable days of my podcasting career is the day a friend of mine, Brian Fullerton, called asking if I would help him with the logistics of starting his own podcast. Brian had a budding YouTube channel, a respected brand, and a rapidly growing social media influence. During that time I was trying my best to crank out podcast episodes while running my lawn care business and also being a radio air-personality in Atlanta. Brian called me out of the blue and I was honored at his request that I help him get his podcast launched. I remember like it was yesterday, as we were talking it was as if the Lord internally shouted to me, "Give him your BEST effort. Show him every tip, insight, important detail, and help him succeed." It was almost as if there was a mandate from heaven, so to speak, to truly help Brian's show reach its full potential. The same energy and effort applied to my podcast was also to be invested helping Brian's new show reach its full potential.

Shortly after Brian hired me to consult and guide his new podcast, he flew me up to Michigan. I helped him set up his new equipment and get set up with all the back-end details to host a professional podcast. Eventually, I got him connected to the best producer in the biz, Mr. Producer, who is my producer as well. Fullerton got my best effort and to this day I continue doing everything possible to help Brian succeed in his podcasting endeavors.

Brian has a rather large following in our industry. He has a lot of respect from key people and he really kind of took me under his wing to help in areas that were not my strengths. He started introducing me to the right people at large companies and the next thing you know doors started flinging wide open. Brand deals and other awesome opportunities began stacking up. When I traced back how everything fell into place, I realized Brian Fullerton helped connect me to the right people at the right time. It was extremely encouraging to see many doors of opportunity opening up for me and how quickly they were opening. I will always be deeply grateful to Brian for his generosity and for taking the time to initiate networking connections with the people he did. In addition to that, he gave me a lot of shout-outs or publicity on his social media that also helped to boost my own podcast and visibility in the lawn care community.

Back to the phrase "It's not what you know it's who you know." In this example, what opened doors for me was not necessarily my knowledge or intellect. It was relationships where there was established trust and credibility. Brian had built relationships with decision-makers over the years and so when he endorsed, promoted, and persuaded companies to do business with me they listened, engaged, and made it happen. They trusted Brian therefore they trusted me. Paul Owens notes, "Be in a constant state of preparation, you never know when it's your time for your thing."

Throughout the pages of this book, the value of integrity, professionalism, relational intelligence and simply treating others the way you want to be treated is continually emphasized. The "It's not what you know it's who you know" concept only works over the course of time where there is a rock-solid foundation of character and trust. Quality people are attracted to quality people.

No, I do not have a man-crush on Brian Fullerton lol. But, here is one more example. I previously mentioned my podcast producer, aka, Mr. Producer, to Brian and he now produces both of our shows. Remember Brian has an impressive directory of relationships, that is to say, a large Rolodex for any of you "OG's" (it seems like anyone in our business who is over thirty-five years of age gets labeled as an Old Guy). One day Brian was chatting with a friend/mentor of his who has a very large social media brand and following. To Brian's surprise, this mentor had listened to the *Fullerton Unfiltered Podcast* and was very impressed with the overall production value and sound quality. You can guess where this is going...

Brian's mentor also hosts a podcast in addition to his gigantic YouTube channel. He expressed to Brian he was currently dissatisfied with his sound engineer/producer and inquired to learn more about who Brian used? That opened the door for Mr. Producer (who already established trust and credibility) to have the incredible opportunity to start a trial period with this new big fish. Of course, Mr. Producer knocked it out of the park with this excellent work and to this day continues to serve this client. What made it all happen? Relationships and networking. (If you want to hire Mr. Producer to do any podcast production or voice-over work for you his contact information will be included at the end of the book).

Now, the danger in all of this is falling into a trap or tendency to hyper-focus on who we know and what they can do for us. This is an extreme danger because if we start to view people in that regard there can be many negative consequences. It is better just to put our heads down, do the right thing, and let these types of doors open naturally, organically, and often in an unexpected way. If you try to force open the door prematurely it can often do more damage than good. Letting things evolve at the right timing and mature in the right way is always better.

I shared a version of this story in my previous book *Cut That Grass and Make That Cash*. If you have followed my podcast for a while you know that in my first lawn care business I serviced many NFL players, coaches, etc… This all happened because I was in the right place at the right time and someone took notice of our high-quality work, attention to detail, and professionalism.

It was a hot summer week in Georgia and we were putting in sod. Little did I know the Atlanta Falcons Defensive Coordinator and his wife were neighbors of our clients. In the evening "Coach Smith" and his wife Renee would take a walk in the neighborhood and they would notice the progress we were making on this front yard makeover. They also took note of the other neighbor's property that we were maintaining and doing some enhancement work on. I vaguely remember them walking by, but what was happening is we were giving them a positive impression. Some time passed, and I later learned they had grown weary of how their current lawn care service was cutting corners and not providing all the services they were promised. And in a near-perfect storm of events, I met Coach Smith and his wife and they decided to hire my company. It was actually weeks later that I discovered Mr. Smith was the Defensive Coordinator. He and his wife would eventually open so many doors for my business to service other coaches, coordinators, the head coach, captain of the team, and many other wealthy neighbors. It was one of the biggest blessings of my career and life.

Now I do not want to make myself sound like a hero. In these examples, the emphasis is on how Brian Fullerton and Coach Smith opened doors for me that changed my life. The outcome was positive. But, I could also share some of my mistakes as there were times I tried too hard to force open doors, make stuff happen, and even worse having the wrong people on the bus. I am a big fan of Jim Collins' book, *Good to Great*. In this excellent book, Collins develops the concept of first who, then what. He explains that great organizations get the right people on the bus.

Now, there were many wrong people that I had on the bus. I was hyper-focused on the destination or what Collins would call the what. Fixated on making progress and getting my business to where I wanted it to be that I neglected the who. I ignored yellow and red flags with some people overlooking their character flaws and thinking if they just get the job done it will be ok. Eventually, their poor decisions and lack of character were causing great harm to my operation. Could I blame them for their lack of integrity, character, relational intelligence, etc? Perhaps, but at the end of the day, I have to own my mistakes and realize I made the poor decision to do life and business with people who did not share my work ethic or values. I let them on the bus. If you have not already read Collins's book I would recommend reading or listening to the audiobook version of *Good To Great* as he explains further how great organizations always think first about who then about what.

In summary, connecting with quality people creates nearly endless possibilities and opportunities. In addition to networking, we need to be on our guard to protect our name and reputation so others can safely trust us. When we are faithful in the little, typically the doors will naturally open for us to have a shot to be faithful with more.

Reflection Questions:

Who has opened doors for you?
What doors can you open for others?

4

Focus on the Family

A couple of the most refreshing and inspiring podcast episodes to date on the Green Industry Podcast are with Andy Mulder from Mulder Maintenance and Services (MMS). Andy's business services Northwest Indiana as they specialize in premier landscaping and hardscaping. With a focus on precision, MMS has created some stunning outdoor spaces. You can check out their impressive portfolio of work on Instagram @mulderoutdoors.

Dave Ramsey explains that when you can get out of debt, it changes your decision-making, your relationships, your future, and your family tree. Andy testified to this as he shared on episode #361 that recently he and his wife paid off their mortgage and are now 100% debt-free both personally and in their business. This impressive feat took them nine years and Mulder said about the challenging process of becoming debt-free, "To be able to pay off your house takes a lot of perseverance and you have to want it really badly! And even in business, I have found it is so easy to want the next thing, and the next piece of equipment and this and that and I want it now. Instagram makes that so hard because you are always looking at what other people have. So having a good why is important. Why do you want to become debt-free? What is it going to do for you? We really think it has given us the freedom to do things we have never done." Andy goes on to explain that now that his family and business are debt-free, the money worries have alleviated and he is able to focus on enjoying more quality time with his family.

One of the components of Andy's story that is very impressive is his intentionality to serving his family. Now that Andy has more margin in his life, he prioritizes Saturdays as a family day with a unique emphasis on making sure he spends quality time with his children on Saturdays. He has nicknamed the day, "Daderday" and said that being home with the family on Saturdays has changed his life. The concept has actually inspired other entrepreneurs such as Joshua Sutton to carve out Saturdays as a day set apart for undivided attention with family. Mulder said, "What do I really want, and how am I going to get there?" For Andy, he wants to have a healthy, strong vibrant relationship with his wife and children. And he believes spending quality time with each of them is part of the path to making those healthy relationships a lasting reality.

In addition to scheduled quality time, Andy believes that clear communication is key to a healthy marriage. In episode #367 Andy shares how he and his wife worked through their conflicts of unmet expectations. Andy's wife was expecting him home for dinner most nights with the family and often Andy would call and notify his wife he had to run out to meet with a client to give a quote. Well, his wife was expecting him home and so this wrench in her plans was problematic. Thankfully, Andy and his wife worked together to come up with a creative solution.

Andy blocked off Tuesday and Thursday evenings from 5:30 - 8:30 pm for meetings with clients. This way his wife could expect that on those two evenings Andy might not be home until later in the evening. But, on the other nights, he scheduled that for family time. So that way he was able to schedule his meetings with clients on Tuesdays and Thursdays and there were no more "surprises" where his wife's expectations were unmet. This simple tweak to Andy's schedule was a game changer and it improved his marriage. In episode #367 Andy said, "I don't want to get to the end of my life and wished I worked more. I'm not going to wish I worked more. I'm just not. Nobody says that when they're sitting there for the last couple of days. Man, I wish I would have put one more hardscape job in the ground. No, I wish I would have spent more time with my children. I think that gets lost in business ownership. If we want to better our lives it's not all about the money."

This is a trait of those who are really flourishing. They realize that business ownership is not only about the financial victories. The winning with money is only part of the equation. The margin from prosperity then gives you the opportunity to really enjoy, cultivate and cherish meaningful relationships. Throughout the two episodes interviewing Andy he continued to reiterate how important getting out of debt is because that really helps free up your time and money to focus on the family. He said, "If you want to have true peace and you don't want to worry about things and you want to be able to make more money than you have ever made, get rid of the things that are taking all your money."

Jason Creel is another guest we have had on the Green Industry Podcast who highly values these relationships. Jason's story is well documented throughout several episodes on the Green Industry Podcast as well as on his YouTube channel, *Lawn Care Life*. Jason has built and sold two lawn care businesses and now is on his third business with a specialization in fertilizer and weed control. What impresses me about Jason and his wife Traci is not only are they victorious financially in the business but they, just like the Mulder's are very intentional about their family thriving.

Recently, I took a little road trip to sweet home Alabama to catch up with the Creels. They have 4 beautiful acres in Trussville and are remodeling their home. What fascinated me throughout my day-long visit at the Creel's was not all the new fancy upgrades to the house but it was the genuine love and peace that was in the atmosphere. My friend Dr. Frank Holleman joined me on the road trip and as we drove back to Atlanta the evening after hanging out at the Creel's, we both reminisced about what a wonderful experience we had with them that day. It was so refreshing to see a family unit operating in God's will and design. The kids were full of joy, the property was full of peace and everything seemed so pleasant. Jason and Traci put in the effort to create this oasis of love, joy, and peace. Their example is a great encouragement to work hard and win in our businesses so we can enjoy the fruit of our labor with our loved ones.

Reflection Question:

What is your plan to improve valuable relationships in your life?

5

The Diligent Shall Prosper

The wise and prudent look ahead to the future. They carefully consider the long-term consequences of current decisions. There is wisdom in thinking before acting. Creating a plan and executing on that blueprint is a trait of high achievers.

To date, our most downloaded episode of the Green Industry Podcast is episode #200 where Brian and Liz Fullerton share their inspiring story about how they paid off a massive amount of debt then eventually saved up money to go from a hideous one-bedroom apartment to building a custom home on their dream property. This story is noteworthy and emphasizes the importance of writing down measurable goals and then working with focus and diligence to accomplish those goals.

We will pick up the story as Liz tells of the night she ripped up the family's goals and cried herself to sleep. Just a heads up, you may want to grab a box of tissues before continuing to read this story.

Liz Fullerton:

It's actually really funny because, in the kitchen, we have a vision board that we look at every single day. It has photos that represent dreams. Sometimes there are tangible things like physical items. And then other times they're just more a representation of what we're trying to do. And we also have a goal card that we read every single day. And if you look at that board, there's actually a sandwich baggie with a bunch of ripped-up paper in it.

In our old apartment, we didn't have the money to even buy a physical vision board to put our dreams on. So we used our refrigerator with magnets. This apartment was a gross place and we couldn't have anybody over.

At this time, friends of ours were having their second kids. It's really hard as a lady when all my friends have houses and kids and the like, one day I'll get there. I'm gonna be 40 by the time that happens, it was hard. I actually ripped up all of our dreams. We had a fight, we had a huge fight.

I ripped up all of the dreams on our refrigerator and laid on my kitchen floor and just sobbed because I just wanted out of that place so badly. And I knew it was gonna happen. But I knew it was going to take longer than what we wanted. And it was really, really hard. And Brian came in and he just held my hand and he said, "Look, we're gonna do it, we're gonna figure it out. It's gonna be okay. This is what I'm doing. This is what I'm tangibly doing. These are the steps."

So he sat there and he held my hand and I stopped crying and we talked about all of the steps that we were taking to get us to where we want it to go and then that's when I got really on board and super excited because then I felt I could tangibly do something to help him further. Our journey and our dreams. I felt like I was on the boat with him. We got both oars going now and we took a sandwich baggie and we put all of those ripped-up dreams in the baggie.

Brian Fullerton:

No! You went to bed, and you were mad and upset. You cried yourself to sleep. And I went back into the kitchen. I'm crying right now. I went back to the kitchen and I saw it wasn't just a piece of paper, it said, the Fullerton Family House 2020. And this was in 2018.

2020 seemed so far away but I say we're gonna build this custom home. It's going to be beautiful. It's going to be amazing. I was working so hard. I already was laying the foundation for the skyscraper. Between the lawn care company and the media company. I'm going to build this thing. I was painting the vision every single day but you saw it, but you just weren't believing it and I'm working so hard. I already see it. I've already bought this home, this is a done deal.

I remember coming around the kitchen, we had these crappy old wooden cabinets, 14-year-old carpet with mystery stains on the carpet. You would vacuum or do the carpet cleaning then the mystery stain would come back in about 12 hours, like that kind of mystery. I remember walking around into the kitchen because we had this horseshoe thing. And I just saw all these pieces of paper on the floor. They represented a home that we wanted back then, this beautiful home on this ranch, on this land, exactly what we're going to build right now. It's just like I get chills, kind of talking about it. And I just saw these little pieces of paper. So I picked them all up, I put them in a little bag and I put a magnet... (inaudible, Brian starts crying).

Liz Fullerton:

He put them back on the refrigerator in the sandwich baggie. So when I walked out and saw that I had a little breakdown, it was kind of like the breakdown we needed to get on the same page because after that you involve me way more in the business. Yeah, you let me contribute basically because it was hard because, when I came around, you had already owned the business for what seven years?

Brian Fullerton:

No, no, ten years. This technically is our 15th season. So it was one of those things where I'm like, it's working, we're putting money in the bank, but I saw, we had on our whiteboard on one side of it was all of our dreams and goals. But the other side was this whole square box, I took a little tiny black electrical tape on my whiteboard and I made what looks like a sales board that you would see at a sales company. I had a Bank of America, Visa, you know, $105 a month, $4,000 balance, 7.9% APR. I learned from Robert Kiyosaki how to get out of debt, how to organize my finances, and then underneath it was Infiniti G37, my sedan we owed $7,500, $305 a month payment, 34 months left, 3.9% interest.

I had all these bills and every month I would update the board. The balances are going down by whatever they were per month. You see it tapering, so I said by 36 months this is done, 24 months this is done, 18 months this is done. At the time I had my Brian's Lawn Maintenance 2.0 setup that a lot of people saw, that red F150 and my old utility trailer and I said look, we have to re-up everything.

We have to buy a new truck, a new mower, a new trailer. I have to drop literally $100,000 on new stuff and we'll pay it off in 36 months and she's like I don't want to buy more stuff I want a home, I want kids. I say if we get the home the kids will always make $50,000 a year from this business. I said but if I drop $100,000, I'll make $200,000 with this thing. We can gross $200,000 in the next like 24 months. So we can grow this business.

I wanted to reinvest, you wanted the upfront material things and by the way, I don't say you don't deserve it, you deserve it. I was already spinning this dream for three or four years. And then what happened was we paid off all the debt. It took a little while to get there. But once we were able to do that, I was like yo now we're cash-flow positive. And that was about 24 months.

Liz Fullerton:

Here's something I kept saying, I don't want to buy a luxury handbag and be broke. That was one of the big things actually when we were getting out of debt. I really love handbags. I've always loved handbags. I love shoes. But, just when we decided we were going to re-up the business, we were going to reinvest and then eventually get out of debt. We couldn't do everything at the same time. I decided that I would sell all my handbags. I bought one tote bag that I knew would last me for a few years. I refused to buy another bag while we were in debt.

Brian Fullerton:

That's what you see around here: all your friends have Louis Vuitton bags. I told Liz, I'm not going to fake it. I'm not going to have a Louis Vuitton bag or some Escalade that's got a $1200 a month payment. Look, if we're gonna do this, we're gonna do it, right.

And we did, we listened to Dave Ramsey, Robert Kiyosaki, and Grant Cardone. And we made our own philosophy on how we wanted to approach our finances. So we had this, this hybrid plan. Look, I need to bring more in and pay a bunch off, I said, I can't pay a bunch off unless I bring a gob more in. So the attitude was, we're going to reinvest everything, then we can make a gob of a gob. Then I'm going to pay off debt because it'll be the easiest thing to do because I have so much coming in.

Liz Fullerton:

And then that's when it started to get really cool, because you would come home at the end of the day and be like, okay, we can cross another debt off of the whiteboard. And I mean, this whiteboard was bigger than our TV. It's massive. All of our debts were written down there. And he would tell me, okay, well change this one to this number. And we can completely cross this one-off because that one's done. And we would leave it up there. So slowly, you saw this bar graph of things getting blacked out as we went.

Brian Fullerton:

And what did I do? I gave you the marker. Yeah. I said, Hey, why don't you go take this blue marker? I said, go cross off this one. And you would cry, I would cry.

Liz Fullerton:

I think half of the time we were so tired and emotionally, just overdrawn on all of our energy tap-outs. And so I cried a lot.

Brian Fullerton:

There was a period about 18 months ago, where I gave you the blue marker, and I said, Hey, you see Bank of America credit cards? Yeah. I said, Hey, why don't you take this marker and go cross it off. And she goes, "You think?" I go, it's done. And I would pull up my phone. It says like payments submitted $3,817 because I had a $4,000 line of credit. And I had that for two years. And it was all business debt. I maxed out credit cards, lines of credit. I had $20,000 to put down on the truck. I was just trying to grow.

We wanted to get out of debt before we had kids. We wanted to get out of that before we built the home. And so then it was five months later, I'm like, Hey, you see that? You know, Sheffield Financial for the trailer payment. The trailer was $9,977, and I had paid off two years of payments. It was a four-year note. But after two years, I only made $1,800 progress. So it was $6,700. I said, Hey, why don't you go walk up to the board, to Sheffield Financial. I opened up my phone and the little mobile payment of $6,750 paid off.

They share a message, thank you so much. And then the next email that says, "thank you so much for your business in this loan, your loan has been recognized as fulfilled. Thank you for the partnership. If you ever need any more options, call or email us, we'd love to service you and serve you." Liz goes off crying, so what was happening was $130 a month servicing on the credit card. I was able to snowball that into the trailer and by the way, we were working hard and making like gobs, we are making $5,000, $10,000, $5,000, $10,000…

Liz Fullerton:

Everything we had other than bills went to paying it off. We ate rice and beans.

Brian Fullerton:

We were still living below our means because we started getting the lawn care business to $12,000 - $18,000 a month coming in. Then my YouTube channel started making a couple of bucks, which we never really lived on or touched. But so far that's been just stacking up. We haven't touched it for four years and we've only really been making money with our YouTube channel for the last 12 months.

The snowball thing started happening. So we got rid of the Visa, we got rid of the trailer, we got rid of another credit card then it was the $21,000 note. And I probably had $7,000 or $8,000 left on it because this was two years into the 42 months. And it was $503 a month. It felt like we're paying more for mower payments than we are for our rent.

Liz Fullerton:

We've had some really low points. But Brian's said it for years now. The only people that get hurt on the roller coaster are the people who jump off and if you just stay and stick it out it does pay off.

Brian Fullerton:

That basically was our story for about this 24-month window at that old apartment, paying off debt, growing the business, we wouldn't pay off debt until we were growing the business first. My attitude was I'm going to make this six-figure cash-flowing machine.

The YouTube channel, I am going to build the biggest lawn care YouTube channel because I have people doubting and I've told this on so many episodes. I had people doubting that you could even grow a YouTube channel or lawn care channel who wants to watch that?

Liz Fullerton:

We know what it takes. I've seen a lot of people say, just in general about you, Brian, and just other creators, how do you run a legit business? If you're doing all this media stuff with YouTube or whatever? Obviously, you can't be putting that much into your business? I'm sorry if you're lazy, and that's the expectation you have in your life. But yeah, you know what, freakin work. You work five days a week on the lawn care, business, whatever. And then you come home and yeah, you're up until 3 am. And people are like, Well, why would you ever do that? Because we have bigger dreams than just having a lawn care business and like not putting anything else out into the world. If you can make yourself successful, that's great. But if you can help other people, that's what makes it worthwhile to me. Why only feed your own mouth if you could teach other people how to feed themselves too.

Paul Jamison:

Where did you purchase your vision board? What would you recommend to someone who wants to create a vision board and goal cards? Where do you start?

Liz Fullerton:

Honestly, the corkboard that we have up there, it's just a corkboard with thumbtacks. It is from Target. I think it was like $15. It doesn't have to be expensive. Like I said, we used to use our refrigerator. So it doesn't have to be anything special. But it needs to be something that's in your face every single day. So don't put it like an inside door of your closet where you rarely see it. We have two copies of that goal card. One is by our coffee maker so I can read it every morning while I'm waiting for my coffee to get made. And then we have one and he taped onto the inside of our shower. Cuz if you're standing in your shower anyway, waiting for your shampoo to wash your hair, read your goals, put your mind on it every single day.

I thought it was so corny, honestly. Because Brian had been doing this for a while when we had met and he said, "No, we have to put our dreams up."

What? That's so weird. And it seems so unattainable at the time, too. It felt so naive to be putting a dream of a house when we can't even afford a better apartment. It just felt so weird. So I did it. And I've seen it happen in our life, and it's crazy you need to be careful. Because if you put something up there, and you're not paying attention to the details, like your mind's fixated on it, it's going to take you there.

Brian Fullerton:

It's funny because I'm in the process of this. So it's like happening to me as well. And literally, as we speak. I was in the shower the other day, so I have a glass door shower, and so we taped the same goal card to the outside of the shower. I was reading the goal card, it wasn't even like a week ago. And I'm going through it and then I read we will hit this many subscribers on your YouTube channel and make this much money and then we will have a live event, we'll have this many people at it. So we're building this dream. We have like 20 different items on there. Where people lack vision, the people are going to perish.

Liz Fullerton:

We were talking about that on the podcast we did together a while ago about the rowboat. You have your life in the boat you're sitting in, and you're trying to get to this island across the way, right? And you can work as hard as you want that one oar in the boat. That's your working effort. The other oar in the boat is your vision. If you don't have any vision, that's your compass, how do you know where you're going?

Brian Fullerton:

Well, and the other part of it is I was reading the actual vision goal card in the shower. In the next 12 to 18 months, Liz and I will close on a five-acre parcel of land. It'll be a perfect property for us to build our dream home. And I'm just reading it because I just am going through the motions, right? I'm just reading it. And I was like, I'm under contract right now for this property!

Liz Fullerton:

It's so wild! And there are certain things that we put on there too. For example, it will be a blessing/favor deal for us. When we find it we will know. When you put in the offer for the land, they went down on the price before we even put an offer in. We put a lower offer than asking and got it!

Just crazy stuff that we spoke and your subconscious mind fixates on it. That's what your brain feeds on all day. It's what it works on all day. It's why they say never to listen to something negative before you go to bed because your mind just dwells on it all night. So yeah, we're a little crazy about the vision and keep it right in front of us because it's so important.

It doesn't always have to be tangible physical items either like we have a picture of a woman praising with her child and to me that represents raising our kids properly how we feel in our faith. You can put anything you want in there but just make sure it's a heartstring thing don't put arbitrary yeah stuff up there.

Brian Fullerton:

The bottom line is I just hope that we try to inspire people. Entrepreneurship is lonely. Period, case closed. It's lonely, you're in the desert. Sometimes you just buy equipment reinvesting, buying equipment, reinvest and grow and grow and you don't get to draw from that company because you got to build the foundation. It's the goose that lays the golden eggs. And if you starve the goose, you're not gonna have the golden eggs. A very simple formula but it's one of those things to where it might take you two, five, twenty years. For me, it was about twelve years for my company to actually get it producing a strong enough income for us. Strong is relative right? But it was a great income for us.

A transparent dream that came true for me, nobody's ever heard this before. But my mom has been working for 50 years, she's 68 years old. And she was working for my uncle as a cabbie. So she wasn't picking up dudes at the bar at 2:00 am like a drunk cabbie, but she was like a courier during the day. She would take medical documents or medical prescriptions or help people get to the airport, she would choose cabbying during the day because she loves interacting and meeting new people.

Well, long story short, because of COVID. Nobody was driving, right? So my uncle's cab business went to a screeching halt. And my uncle came to this crossroad, like does he pay? I think it's $13,000 a year in insurance to insure one car, which is insane. And so the business was starting to go downhill. And so my mom got laid off.

So I said, Mom, How much does it take to make you stay at home? What is that going to cost? So we looked at her finances. She's out of debt. She's put some money in the bank.

And she gave me a number and I said, Hey, congratulations. I'm gonna put you on my payroll, we'll take care of you. And you'll never work another day of your life. And when Liz and I have a baby, I want you to be a full-time grandma.

. . .

To hear the whole conversation with Brian and Liz you can take a listen to episode #200 on the Green Industry Podcast. As I sat in their living room on that Sunday afternoon recording the podcast I was getting so fired up. Their story of having clear goals, making sacrifices, working together, and sticking with it until accomplishing their goals is inspiring.

Reflection Questions:

What are your dreams? What are your measurable goals to get from here to there?

6

A Formula That Really Works

One of the most frequently asked questions we receive at the Green Industry Podcast is how do you find good employees? Recruiting and retaining good employees is essential to the long-term success of our operations. Let's explore what businesses are doing that have a good record with employee retention.

In the lawn and landscape industry, motivating somebody to show up to work long hours in various weather conditions while doing labor-intensive work can be challenging. Just last night a friend who owns a large service-based business with several employees texted me that he's considering selling his business because he can't handle dealing with the labor crisis anymore. The stress of trying to find and keep employees is becoming too much and he is actually considering selling his business and working in a completely different industry.

Troy Clogg and Associates continuously ranks as a top landscape and snow and ice management company. I was curious about what their strategy is to have the right employees on their team. While out on our first annual Summer Road Tour back in the Summer of 2020 I stopped by their headquarters to check out their operation.

When I arrived at their headquarters, the owner, Troy Clogg was in a meeting with some bankers. One of his team members, Adam greeted me at the front door. Immediately I remember seeing some life in Adam's eyes. I sensed it was beyond hospitality or just trying to help me have a solid first impression of their business. I recognized it was genuine. As he gave me a tour of their headquarters it was obvious Adam was truly passionate about working there. Then, I met another team member, he had been there for over 25 years. Same countenance, same passion. These two seemed to have a merry heart and gratitude for their job. Continuing to chat it was apparent they actually liked where they worked. It was beyond just a reliable paycheck. They felt important and like their work mattered.

After touring their impressive headquarters I sat down with the owner Troy Clogg to interview him for my podcast. This episode can be found way back in the archives, Episode #202. Right out of the gate in the interview, I asked Troy, what is it about this place that your employees seem so energetic and thankful to work here? Without hesitation, Troy replied, "Culture."

Prompting Troy to explain how he and his management team created this successful culture he answered, "It's a reflection of the ownership and leaders. Passion is important. Lots of people go to work. We spend more time as an average American at work than we do at home, so you gotta love what you do and surround yourself with people who are like-minded that do passionately like their work. You have to stand for something more than cutting grass, plowing snow, and doing patios or whatever the case may be."

Troy went on throughout the rest of that episode to explain that most of our society does not even know what their foundation is. They know they don't like this guy or that guy right now because of this or that but they don't really know their foundation. Clogg explained that his foundation is based on his faith and a long-term plan and that his company's purpose is to transform lives. Troy focuses on trying to inspire others to be better tomorrow than they are today.

Other companies I've had the privilege of visiting and working with share similarities and have common threads in their company culture. One such example is Kohler which is best known for its plumbing products, but the company also manufactures furniture, cabinetry, tile, engines, and generators.

The team at Kohler Engines hosted an impressive event in February of 2020. The event was located in Hattiesburg, Mississippi where Kohler

Engines has a gigantic manufacturing facility that we toured. The facility was impressive but what was even more impressive was the gratitude and appreciation the folks at Kohler had for their opportunity to have a career at Kohler. I was blown away when those I interviewed from the Kohler team shared the duration of how long that had been with the company. They had each been with the company for quite some time and several of them even had family members that put in 30+ years with Kohler and are now retired. That track record of unusual employee retention had me intrigued. How does Kohler achieve such incredible employee retention? How are they recruiting and retaining such quality people?

Recently after a workout at the gym, I stopped by their front office where they have a huge freezer where you can buy pre-made healthy meals. As I was examining what meals looked good, I witnessed an interesting brief conversation. A gym member had just walked through the door and said hello to the gym worker who was assisting me with my food order. The incoming member greeted the worker with a simple, "Hello, how are you doing?" The gym worker replied, "I am doing well thanks for asking, how are you?" The woman quickly answered back, "I'm doing good, thanks." As the member was on her way to the other end of the gym, the gym worker looked at me with a grin and said "I don't really think she is doing well. You can see it all over her body language. She is not having a good day at all." I actually noticed the same thing. The countenance on the woman's face as well as the rest of her body language did not match her words that she was doing good. This lady who just entered the gym looked uptight, tense, even a little furious. But, she said she was doing good and put on what was perceived to be a fake smile.

I think that is how a lot of employees at companies are. They say they are doing good and like their job but the truth is they don't really like waking up Monday morning to go to work. They just need the paycheck so they show up, go through the motions, say the right things, and collect the paycheck. For these employees, their internal reality is not truly what they portray outwardly.

However, this was not the case with the Kohler team members I spoke with. What I noticed with the folks that worked at Kohler was that they legitimately liked working for this company. They had a thankfulness and genuine appreciation to get to be a part of the Kohler team.

This positive attitude carried over to the experience at the event I participated in. After the event concluded, I spoke with many who attended. Literally, 100% of the people I surveyed said they enjoyed their experience at the event and are glad they came. Many spent a lot of money on travel and sacrificed a few days away from their business and families and they thought the event was worth attending. There was something in the atmosphere where you could feel like we were a part of something special which was presented with excellence. There was something bigger going on and we were a part of the story. The team at Kohler made sure everything was organized, world-class, and well run. The attendees noticed the championship culture and enjoyed their time at the event.

Kohler is known for its exceptional kitchen, bath, engine products, and more. But behind those quality products is a team of employees who enjoy being a part of the company that creates absolutely brilliant products. Even though I only experienced the Kohler culture for a couple of days it was enough for me to grasp this was a healthy culture. As we think back to our most frequently asked question at the Green Industry Podcast, how do you find good employees? My observation is that Kohler in part has a great foundation and culture. Here are some of my takeaways of how they have achieved an environment that attracts high-achieving, quality employees.

For starters, they have solid products. Kohler has been making phenomenal products for a long time. You could tell how the Kohler employees were proud of the quality products their company made. Their morale and spirit were delightful and they all seemed to have a strong confidence that they knew they were a part of a world-class company.

Secondly, the Kohler team is well taken care of. Obviously, they did not divulge the specific earnings of each employee or details of their benefits and retirement plans, but I got the picture that they were content and appreciative of their pay, benefits, and work environment. The majority of our audience for the Green Industry Podcast own home service-based businesses and I can hear them fussing saying, "Well, how in the world can I afford to pay my guys more?" I have heard that question again and again. Kohler obviously has the money, margin, and capabilities to treat their team wonderfully. The path to profitability varies from industry to industry but one thing is for sure. The faster you can establish the margin to be able to comfortably take good care financially of your team the better. This is not the end all be all, but it certainly helps boost the mood of employees when they are fairly compensated.

In episode #462 of the Green Industry Podcast AJ and Alicia Brentzel from Brex Enterprises shared about a survey they recently did with their team members. Brex Enterprises is a pipeline maintenance company in Pennsylvania that grosses north of $10,000,000 a year and has over 40 employees. When Alicia asked their team what is the most important reason they work at the business, surprisingly the amount of pay was not the #1 answer. What the team members most appreciated about Brex Enterprises was the opportunity for growth in the company.

This brings me to my third point about what I noticed about the strong Kohler culture and that is they saw a tremendous opportunity for growth in the company. There was not just a little bit of light at the end of the tunnel, but the vision for the future was very bright. If they continued to be reliable and perform well they could expect a promotion or reward. Team members seemed motivated to perform at a high level. Not one of them gave off the vibe they were mailing it in or going through the motions.

An additional takeaway related to their exceptional culture was how organized everything they did was. The event they hosted was flawless and touring their manufacturing plant I noticed how everything was so orderly. When things are organized and clean it creates stability and peace.

A cleaning crew comes by the Green Industry Podcast Studios twice a month. It is typically the same two ladies that come and make the place spotless. I absolutely love coming to work later that day after they cleaned. I open the door and the cheerful fragrance hits me and as I walk in noticing everything is so fresh, tidy, and immaculate. I love when things are clean, organized, and orderly and so do employees.

Back when I was at a low point in the early days of my landscaping business I was chatting with a mentor. He asked me a candid question, "Paul, would you enjoy working at your company, Jamison Landscaping?" I paused before answering and really pondered and then came to a humbling realization. Probably not. First and foremost, it's hard work, cutting that grass, trimming bushes, installing sod and mulch, etc. Day after day it can be gruesome. But beyond the actual physical labor in the elements such as the Georgia heat, my business at that time was disorganized and in many ways amateur. This was a helpful punch in the gut my mentor gave me. Of course, he already knew the answer, but he was helping me to face reality and hopefully make some changes. Thankfully, I did and tried to get things in order and be more professional, systematized, and organized asap.

Our culture today seems like it plays musical chairs with jobs. Jason Creel recently joked on episode #488 of the Green Industry Podcast that he had 15 jobs before finally building his own business Alabama Lawn Pros. He was so unsettled and dissatisfied with his previous work experiences that he literally created his own company. He now has an environment and culture where he wakes up every day excited to go to work. The goal is to create conditions where it is enjoyable to be at your job. Kohler does that well and it shows in their employee retention. I found a similar story at ECHO.

In 2018 ECHO invited a group of landscape and lawn care professionals to a two-day event at their headquarters in Lake Zurich, Illinois. This was a time for a lot of round table talks with other industry professionals as we all discussed the challenges we face as lawn and landscape business owners. Very shortly after arrival at ECHO's superb world headquarters, they took us on a tour of the manufacturing center. The mass-production of their products was quite the sight, but what distinctly caught my attention was the zeal and passion our tour guide had for his company.

He was so proud of the excellence and attention to detail that ECHO puts into the entire assembly-line production process. The eye is the gate to the soul and you could see it in his eyes, he was so proud to be a part of producing high-quality products. It was rather loud on the floor with all the manufacturing going on. We were wearing headsets dialed into a frequency so we could hear the tour guide's commentary as we walked through the facility. I was mesmerized by his body language and the joy he expressed when showing off how ECHO makes their various products. This employee who was leading our group was having a blast showcasing ECHO's production process. Here was another example of an employee who actually likes his job.

Over the course of the next couple of days, I was able to chat with several other folks at ECHO such as their President, Director of Marketing, and many of the product developers. It was the same feeling with each ECHO employee. They liked working at ECHO and took great pride in creating the best possible products. This was a rare experience for me to meet their executives, tour their plant and my takeaway was this culture is stable and very enjoyable. I already knew ECHO had good products but after leaving this event I now knew they also had good employees. There was a clear correlation between their healthy culture and their high-achieving employees.

In retrospect, good employees are attracted to a good culture. I saw this first hand at the Toro Company, Kohler, ECHO where their culture was solid and so are their employees. Of course, their products are good too. But, this also carries over to service-based businesses. I recognized the companies that had good foundations as Troy Clogg put it also had good employees. The result of having a good culture is you put your company in a favorable position to attract the right people on the bus.

Reflection Question

What is your plan to improve company culture?

7

The Trend Is Your Friend

One of the most unique podcast interviews I have conducted is with a YouTuber who had 13,000,000,000 views on YouTube before retiring. You read that correctly thirteen billion. I recently got to hang out with him at his new home and he was showing me his multiple YouTube Gold and Silver Play buttons. You receive a Gold Play button when you hit 1,000,000 YouTube subscribers and a Silver Play when you hit 100,000 subscribers. It was impressive that he had multiples of each. He experienced tremendous success on YouTube. At his peak, he was receiving millions of views a day and was literally ranked the #1 YouTube channel in the world for several weeks in a row.

After interviewing him for the podcast we sat in his kitchen for hours talking about his incredible performance on YouTube. I asked him how he was able to achieve such great accomplishments? A summary of his answers was that it was a mix of comprehensive research, understanding trends, skill, talent, and being at the right place at the right time.

One memorable phrase he shared was, "The Trend is Your Friend." Now, in context, he was referring to the YouTube algorithm and what they were promoting. He would pay close attention to what the algorithm is favoring and promoting? That is a good piece of information to pay attention to and consider when strategizing content and metadata. This concept that the "Trend is Your Friend" is helpful when understanding social media algorithms and also general business as well.

I am not necessarily highlighting the trend of what's popular on TV or the latest TikTok dance etc. I experienced something interesting on Super Bowl Sunday when the Super Bowl was recently hosted by Tampa Bay and the Tampa Bay Buccaneers actually played in the game and won. I just happened to be in Tampa that evening. I was out on the Florida Road Tour for my podcast. And a group of social media influencers was staying at the Green Industry Hype House on delightful Anna

Maria Islands. The Hype House was a big collaboration for influencers to come together for the week to create content and share business tips with each other. It was like a week-long mastermind collaboration epic experience. Since most folks were flying in and I had driven down I was picking up folks from the airport and taking them back to the island. So to clarify I was not in the stands at Raymond James Stadium for the Super Bowl that evening but I did get to experience the Super Bowl traffic experience during my commutes throughout the city that Super Bowl Sunday.

When I picked up my friends Jason and Traci Creel at the airport it was about 6:30 pm. The opening kick had already happened and we had about an hour drive back to Anna Maria Island which included the scenic drive over the Sunshine Sunset Bridge that connects Tampa Bay to St. Petersburg. Jason Creel is a big football fan. He's more of a college football guy as he is a proud supporter of the Alabama Crimson Tide, "Roll Tide Roll!" As we were driving back Jason was saying that he looked forward to joining the "Super Bowl Party" to enjoy watching the second half showdown between Tom Brady vs Patrick Mahomes. Jason was simply assuming we were having a Super Bowl Party.

I had not been back to the Hype House that evening, but I told Jason knowing the folks that are at the house; they are probably not even going to be watching the game. Jason was flabbergasted when I suggested this might be the case. How could you be an American and not watch the Super Bowl? Now, I was born and raised in Canton, Ohio, home of the Pro Football Hall of Fame so I respect the sport and grandeur of the Super Bowl. But, I also knew that the people who are at the Green Industry Hype House are all entrepreneurs and they are going to take advantage of this incredible opportunity to collaborate and share ideas with each other. They are probably preoccupied doing that and they won't even watch the Super Bowl.

When we arrived at the Green Industry Hype House after the gorgeous commute my assumption was right. Nobody in this packed house of energetic entrepreneurs was watching the game. They were talking shop and picking each other's brains about algorithms, what's working and what's not in the social media world, and just enjoying each other's company.

Some people call it tunnel vision. And I have noticed some of the ultra-successful business leaders are able to stay focused on what matters and not get distracted by lesser important issues. And so when my friend says the "Trend is Your Friend" he is saying hone in on industry-specific tendencies. Timing is everything and if you are aware and alert you can position yourself to be in the right place at the right time.

Now Jason was surprised these guys were not watching the Super Bowl and honestly I was astonished too. Typically each year I will watch the Super Bowl, longing for the day the Cleveland Browns make an appearance and perhaps even win it all. But, what intrigued me was a group of entrepreneurs who wanted to gain an edge in their businesses and so they spent that Sunday evening having meaningful conversations about how they can take their business to the next level. They were basically sharing each other's "secrets". I was like a fly on the wall listening to these successful business owners, YouTubers and Instagrammers chat about automation, delegation, thumbnails, content strategy, when to post, how often to publish content, etc. Back and forth they went on and on and I was soaking up every minute. The trend can be your friend if you diligently study the trend and ride the wave to your benefit.

Reflection Questions

What trends have you noticed lately? How can your business benefit from these tendencies?

8

Get The Competitive Edge

O ne of the main goals in my life is to eat healthily and exercise regularly. On Saturday mornings there is a group fitness class at the gym where I am a member. This class not only offers a good workout but also accountability. The other men in this workout group have become friends and they offer a lot of encouragement to continue towards my health and fitness goals.

These Saturday morning workouts are roughly 45 minutes. We each set up our little station including a mat for our core exercises and a combination of a kettlebell and dumbbells for our strength training. There is one athlete in particular who regularly attends. This fellow is tall, shredded, and in fantastic shape. He makes the challenging, strenuous workout look rather easy and routine.

Upon arrival at the class, I intentionally locate where this athlete is setting up his station and attempt to set up my station near him. The Saturday morning workout really is super intense but working out side by side with this athlete who is in tip-top shape pushes me hard. When we get 30 minutes into the workout I usually get extremely tired, but there he is next to me grunting, laser-focused on finishing the workout strong. His tenacity influences me to dial in and keep going, finishing strong, getting the most out of this training session.

These group workouts are way more effective for me than solo workouts. Being in the environment with this group helps me to get phenomenal results and stay focused. The things we need to stay on top of and change often can be assisted when we lean on others for their accountability, guidance, and motivation. The standard is set so much higher in the class and it helps me to take my work out to higher heights. You can do a lot in a short amount of time when you are locked in, concentrating, and go all out. This is also applicable in business.

Russell Skipper is the owner of Solid Green Landscaping in Monroe,

Georgia. Russell has been a guest on the Green Industry Podcast multiple times and I noticed something after each interview. As time goes on Russell's passion for success in his business continues to grow. He is making progress and seems to be on fire in his pursuit of greatness. Russell's results are different from many others in the same industry. What is the reasoning for Russell's exceptional business success?

One major component is that Russell continues to give credit to the mastermind group he is in with several other prosperous small business owners. This group consists of small business owners across the USA and the majority of them do over a million dollars in annual revenues. They communicate regularly and keep each other accountable in their businesses to make sure they are achieving better results.

Russell does pay to be a part of this nationwide mentorship network, but he believes it is worth every penny as it provides his business a good return on investment. The majority of the business owners in this mastermind group are in their 50s and 60s and full of knowledge. Being a part of a mentorship group like this gives Russell the opportunity to check in with at least 3-4 people to help guide him in making major business decisions. Recently, they helped Russell run the numbers and make the appropriate changes to move into a bigger shop. Additionally, they help Russell with decisions on when to hire new employees. They also assist him with marketing decisions and much more.

Even though Russell has a solid business he continues to stretch himself by being intentionally engaged with other small business owners who are much further ahead of him in revenue, profits, and experience. He continues to reiterate to me both on and off-air that having these guys who are further along than him look into his business has been a game-changer. They are able to point out to Russell areas where he can improve. And their friendship and accountability help Russell to then make the appropriate changes to fine-tune his business to perform even better. It's the classic example of iron sharpens iron that guests so often refer to on the Green Industry Podcast. Russell continues to humble himself and put himself in positions to learn from some of the best. He is not complacent thinking he has arrived, but he surrounds himself with those who challenge him to reach his fullest potential. It is the same principle as the workout class. We can achieve better results when we surround ourselves with others who are headed on a similar path. Whether it's improved health or bigger profits, having mentors and accountability helps give us a competitive edge.

Reflection Question:

What are you doing to surround yourself with positive people who challenge you to live a better life?

9

Tweaking Details To Increase Efficiency

Pete Denny from GCI Turf Services and Kyle Perkins from KPS Lawncare and Landscaping both own and operate million-dollar lawn care businesses in North Carolina. Recently, on the 2nd Annual Green Industry Podcast Summer Road Tour, I stopped by each of their headquarters for a visit and to also interview them for the podcast. Pete is located in Reidsville and has about 15 employees while Kyle is in Raleigh and has around 27 employees. Other than the similarities of both Pete and Kyle being born and raised in North Carolina and owning a lawn care business, they both have a noteworthy peculiarity to discovering ways to operate their business with more efficiency. A specific example of this is that both Pete and Kyle have recently changed their entire truck and trailer set up to feature an improved system that makes their employees happier and drives better work efficiency increasing profitability.

The most common setup we see across the lawn and landscape industry throughout the United States is a pickup truck that hauls either an open or enclosed trailer. Here in Atlanta if you pull up to a busy intersection you will likely notice one of these lawn setups. They are the popular norm and there is quite a bit of content out there comparing and contrasting the open trailer vs enclosed trailer lawn care setup. But as Pete and Kyle have discovered just because something is popular doesn't mean it's the most profitable. They actually have recently switched over to a completely different setup.

On a shop tour video I posted on my YouTube channel Pete Denny said, "Of course you have to be efficient to make money." Pete went on in this video to show off his new style setup where the vehicle essentially has the trailer storage area built into the vehicle. Pete explained that his new style setup simplifies things by going to one truck from a truck and a trailer and that makes it easier for his employees to maneuver and drive. Summarizing his transition Pete noted, "They are just more efficient, they are easier, they are safer, they are not pulling a trailer, they got everything sitting right here behind them, and my guys absolutely love this setup."

Pete's countenance brightened up when he explained that his employees love the new style setup. This attribute of the business owner having a genuine concern for their employees' outlook is very common among those who have lasting business success.

While out on the same tour, one of the special guests Alex Kirby hosted me at his parents' gorgeous lake house on the shores of Lake Murray outside of Columbia, SC. This couple is now enjoying retirement as they recently sold the business they built for decades for a nice amount. They were very open to discuss their business story and I was intrigued as they shared the keys to their success. Without hesitation, they recognized that one of their best attributes was having great employee retention. They far exceeded the norm for employee retention in their specific industry. Similar to how Pete's demeanor lit up when he talked about his employees loving his setup, the Kirby's also radiated big smiles when sharing about how their employees had such long tenures with their business. They actually took such delight in the welfare of their employees that even at the sale of the business they made sure when the new ownership took over that the current employees who had been there for years would be well taken care of.

The Kirby's explained how they made sure their employees had the right tools, work environment, and compensation plans that kept them happy and producing at an effective level. What was most noteworthy about this conversation is that the Kirby's were continuously readjusting and revising their business over the years to make sure they were at optimal efficiencies. They stayed ahead of the pack and made sure they were continuously improving efficiency.

From vetting new customers to execution of service to billing and everything in between, increasing efficiency is vital. Frequent assessments and evaluations on our businesses are helping to make sure we are alert, aware, and informed on where we can improve. The bottom line is efficiency impacts our bottom line.

Reflection Question:

What can you do in your business to increase efficiency?

(10)

A Commitment to a Bright Future

The old saying goes, "If it ain't broke, don't fix it." While in some contexts that may be good advice, in other circumstances that is poor advice. As we discussed in the previous chapter Pete is transitioning his truck and trailer setups from the traditional truck pulling a trailer to the new style of an all-in-one vehicle/trailer setup. The conventional setup is not broken. It will get the job done. And for lawn bros and sisters just getting their start, perhaps getting an old F-150 to pull a 5x8 trailer is a less expensive way to enter into the business. But, as Pete reiterated there is a better way for his specific business. Kyle came to the same conclusion for his business as well. But, how did they arrive at the decision to transition their vehicle and hauling setups? The simple answer is education.

The top-notch businesses that I have observed are continuously educating themselves on how they can improve. They do not just make willy nilly, haphazard decisions. But, rather there is a habit of doing research into each detail of the business and how it can improve.

A fun example of this is the process of how Mitchell Gordy recently built his dream shop in Colfax, North Carolina. For years Mitchell had a goal to have a dream shop on a large plot of land. And so Mitchell worked and saved, worked and saved and continued to work and save until he felt it was the right time to build this dream shop.

Mitchell was very deliberate throughout the entire process of building this shop as he ultimately was the General Contractor. On episode #483 of the Green Industry Podcast Mitchell shared his thoughtful approach throughout the building process as he would get a minimum of 2-3 quotes for each different project as the shop was being built. Mitchell was not hasty and did not just hire the first "Chuck in the Truck" claiming to know how to swing a hammer.

Mitchell combined vigilance with caution as he compared contractors' experience, reputation, and price. He gathered as much valuable information as possible to make an informed decision. Whether we are building an expensive shop or a profitable business gathering and studying the appropriate information is important.

Mitchell worked very hard to save up the money to have this opportunity to build this dream shop. He deemed it essential to ensure each penny was invested wisely throughout the building process. At the writing of this book, the shop is entering its final stages of completion and you can actually follow along on Mitchell's YouTube Channel, *Mitchell's Lawn Care LLC*.

The definition of education is the process of receiving or giving systematic instruction or an enlightening experience. In middle school, my teacher escorted the class to the library where librarian Frank Sowers introduced us to the Dewey Decimal System. We would then use that system to locate the particular book we were searching for. At the time it was kind of an interesting treasure hunt. But, with the incredible technological advancements in society, it now seems outdated and clunky.

This oddity of calculating decisions and their effect on the future is common in successful businesses. The good news is nowadays retrieving the necessary information to help us make better-informed decisions is easier than ever. Google will complete our thoughts as we are typing out what we are searching for in the search engine. Within a few seconds, we have access to seemingly unlimited information, for free. While paying for particular educational resources can be very beneficial there is also tons of free information out there that we should consider when building our business.

Practically speaking, it's always good to investigate and explore a business before using its product or service. What are their reviews? No reviews? That could be a huge red flag? Bad or fake reviews? That could be another red flag. Having good social proof is not only wise for our own businesses reputation but it can also tell us a lot about companies we are considering purchasing from.

Whether we are researching what contractor is the right fit for building a property like in the case with Mitchell's dream shop. Or perhaps we are purchasing new equipment or are investigating what customer relationship management software is the best for our specific business, making the effort to become knowledgeable and informed on that topic is a good idea.

Reflection Question:

What information can you gather to help you make better, more informed decisions in the future?

11

Expand Your Business Potential

A popular guest on the Green Industry Podcast is Matt Lamarsh from Sandy Springs, Georgia. Referring to his booming business Matt's often referred to as "La Smash It." For several years Matt had a successful career in Corporate America. Ultimately, however, Matt's entrepreneurial tendencies drove him to transition and launch his own landscaping business. Matt shared the entire story of how he started, grew, and eventually sold Lamarsh Landscaping in episode #83 of the Green Industry Podcast.

Currently, Matt is absolutely crushing it as a real estate agent in the white-hot Atlanta market. Matt is an inspiration to many on social media with his content emphasizing a diligent work ethic and attention to detail in business and life. Recently, on one of his IG stories Matt went off on an epic rant about a deceiving email he received. What upset Matt was that the body of the email did not match the subject line. This disinformation, dishonesty, and deceit really set Matt off. With his unique sense of humor, Matt shared his takeaways of the email in an entertaining and instructional IG story rant.

Matt's main message throughout the multiple IG stories posts was, "DO BETTER"! Winning in business does not have to come through lying and tricks to get the clicks and sales. Matt reiterated if you actually add real value to your customer, you may be surprised by the success to follow. His message was to try to win by doing things the right way and just simply do better.

The Golden Rule is to treat others the way you want to be treated. That is so simple, yet so profound. Do you want to open an email that is a gimmick? No. Do you want to answer your phone and it is some scammer trying to defraud you? No. So why would someone send that or attempt to conduct business this way? The get-rich-quick traps may have upfront gain, but in the long run, they will come back to haunt those who use these forms of manipulation and trickery to build their business.

This principle not only applies to business but also to our personal lives. "The naive believes everything, But the sensible person considers his steps." - Proverbs 14:15. The following story is one of those lessons learned through the school of experience where a close friend of mine did not wisely consider his steps but rather gullibly was deceived by a scammer. Although this mistake cost him some money and emotional pain it was a great lesson learned to carefully consider his steps in the future.

Years ago my buddy Kevin drove a black 2001 Mercedes Benz. The interior was immaculate, but on the exterior, the front hood was beginning to fade. Kevin called a couple of auto body repair shops and one quoted him $800 and the other was about $1,000 for the hood paint job. The raggedy hood did bother him and so he had it on his eventual to-do list of future expenses.

One night while Kevin was at his restaurant job at TGI Fridays waiting tables, he had a dinner guest sit at his table who was telling him he did auto body repairs. Kevin mentioned to him he had received a couple of quotes for his hood ranging from $800-$1,000 and the dinner guest scoffed in disgust when hearing those rates. Mr. "repairman" told Kevin without hesitation he would get him taken care of for a much lower price. Curiously Kevin asked him how much? He replied, "$230, You give me your VIN, I'll order the right paint and we can get this done tomorrow."

Do you ever get a gut check? It's like the Holy Spirit is whispering or sometimes it may seem like shouting, "something's not right here, something's off." Well, Kevin said he instantly had that feeling that something was off, but unfortunately, he ignored that initial warning, and this guy's bullying personality was persuading Kevin to move forward with this seemingly too good to be true paint job.

The next red flag was he told Kevin to meet him in a public parking lot. Kevin thought to himself why don't we meet at his shop? Does he even have a shop? What kind of auto body repair guy is this? Instead of being prudent and giving thought to his steps as Proverbs suggests, Kevin mistakenly agreed to meet him at the parking lot at a local shopping center.

Upon arrival, Kevin paid him the $230 cash and the repairman took a can of spray paint and sprayed Kevin's rusted, faded hood. It took him no more than five minutes as he seemingly carelessly sprayed the hood. At this point, Kevin was getting very concerned and started drilling him with questions. Kevin was no expert in painting a hood, but it seemed like there had to be a little more detail or precision involved? The repairman went on to tell lie after lie. Kevin was feeling uncomfortable the whole time, but the repairman continued to reassure Kevin that after it dries it will look great and match the rest of the vehicle. He told Kevin to just give it a few days and assured him if there were any issues to call him and he will make sure Kevin is happy with the result after it dries.

So a few days passed and literally the hood looked worse than before he sprayed it. He told Kevin he got the exact paint on the original vehicle but Kevin thought he just picked up the cheapest can of black spray paint at the big box store. Now, Kevin was out $230 and his vehicle looked worse than before. Of course, when Kevin called him, he did not answer. Kevin sent texts, but no reply. Kevin left him several voicemails and he never responded to any of Kevin's communications. It turned out the repairman was a lying scammer. Finally, Kevin just gave up, forgave him, and cut his losses.

I'm not sure whatever happened to that guy, but if Kevin ever did run into him again I would imagine Kevin would tell him to do better. Both parties involved in that situation should have done better. Let's start with the scam artist "repairman". He may have got a quick $230 and only spent $8 in cost on a can of spray paint, but I doubt he sleeps well at night. And he certainly did not get any referrals from Kevin and he never showed up at TGI Fridays again. That is no way to live life. You reap what you sow and unfortunately for this fellow eventually his actions and dishonesty will likely catch up with him.

Then there is Kevin. He should have done better. He ignored those promptings of concern that he should not do business with this guy. Did Kevin check the repairman's social proof online by analyzing his reviews etc? No, he did not. Kevin let the repairman's high-pressure manipulation persuade him. It did teach Kevin a good lesson though about taking time to study up to become more knowledgeable in order to make better decisions. Also, remember in chapter seven how Russell Skipper checks in with 3-4 mentors before making a major decision? Well, an example of a $230 decision perhaps Kevin did not need wise counsel from 3-4 people. Even if he would have checked in with one other business leader they would have probably noticed this was a dumb idea and tell him to run to the hills where his help comes from.

In summary, when you provide a good service at a fair price and consistently meet/exceed your customer's expectations over time there should be success. But these folks who are a flash in the pan come and go. Their poor work and dishonesty are laying the foundation for a crash. These are the folks that go out of business and are on to the next thing. But, those who actually do better and serve their customers well can sleep like a baby at night and enjoy the fruit of their labor. The Golden Rule is such a good compass for not just life but also business dealings. Treat others the way you want to be treated.

Reflection Question

What is one thing you could do better in your business?

12

Experience All The Benefits of Relational Intelligence

Now that we have established how crucial networking and quality character is, it is important to discuss what to do and not to do when it comes to cultivating relationships. A consistent trait of the business leaders who are achieving great success is that they seem to be in the right place at the right time. Their reoccurring stories of this happening are stunning. Are these folks just super lucky? Or perhaps Zig Ziglar explains how this happens when he shared, "Success occurs when opportunity meets preparation."

Before starting the Green Industry Podcast I was an on-air personality at an Atlanta radio station. It was a part-time job and in hindsight, it was also broadcasting experience and training that would be beneficial years down the road in podcasting. This was also the time when forming the connection with "Mr. Producer" who has been a huge blessing to the landscape podcast community.

My deejay career all started on what we called the Night Watch. It was the midnight - 6:00 am shift. My buddy Bruce would work a few nights a week and I would work the other nights. Collectively we made sure the radio station was live 24/7 by covering the most challenging shift, the overnight shift aka the "graveyard shift." After what seemed like an eternity being on the overnight shift the General Manager eventually promoted me to the 10:00 am - 2:00 pm shift.

One year in September, a group of the executives at the station took a trip overseas. All the "bosses" were all gone. They left the station to a few of the on-air personalities to manage while they enjoyed their international trip. I remember the many emails while they were on their trip. The emails were crafted kindly and professionally but the messaging was the same, "Stay in your lane." I could predict the emails, there would be some key points to make sure logistically the station is up and running while the leadership was overseas and then the email would end with the friendly reminder, "Stay in your lane."

Of course, I did my best to diligently stay in my lane. I did exactly what I would do even if the bosses were in town. And thankfully they had clearly identified what, "stay in your lane" meant. They clearly outlined what we were to say while on air, what should not be said, how long my segments should be, what events to promote, etc... The instructions were clear.

When it comes to relationships, unfortunately, many folks did not "get the memo". What are the instructions? In business, what is appropriate? What is proper to say? To whom? How often? What does it mean to stay in your lane in the context of business relationships? To whom and in what scenarios is it best just to keep our mouths shut?

Thankfully, in seventh grade, I received some good training on relational intelligence when beginning my very first job at Congress Lake Country Club in beautiful Hartville, Ohio. Congress Lake was a gorgeous private golf course that had a highly respected caddy program. It was like Bushwood Country Club in the movie *Caddyshack*, just a little bit more high class. This caddy program was known for producing superb caddies as well as for the college scholarships they would give to the top-achieving caddies.

It was difficult to get hired at Congress Lake. You essentially needed to "know someone." Thankfully, a friend from school knew someone and was able to help me get the job. Before actually starting on the bag as a caddy you must pass Caddy School. This included classroom and on-course training. Before they took us out on the course for training they started with the classroom training in the illustrious clubhouse. We gathered in this elegant room that looked like an expensive library you would see in the movies. The furniture was so nice in this room I didn't even want to sit in it. But, they had us all sit down at this super expensive table and that's when Mr. Olsen walked into the prestigious room.

Mr. Olsen was a long-time member of the club and he was going to lead us new caddies through schooling alongside the Caddy Master. Mr. Olsen began his presentation by explaining to us how exclusive the club was and how the members needed to be honored and valued. He explained how important it was that we treat them with dignity and reverence. When the members retreated to the club they were expecting to be treated in a world-class manner and so Mr. Olsen explained how we were to serve the members to make sure they felt special and appreciated.

This was essentially free education on relational intelligence as Mr. Olsen shared this insightful guidance with the aspiring caddies. At the time I was too immature to appreciate just how valuable this information was, my mind was more preoccupied with eventually getting to play golf on this fine course. They had a policy if you caddied one round over the weekends then you got to golf for free at Congress Lake on Mondays while the course was closed to members. This course was so immaculate and my imagination was already thinking ahead to the days I would get to golf there on Mondays.

Mr. Olsen explained to us that the members were affluent and our job was to deliver exceptional service to them before, during, and after their round of golf. The Caddy Master would interject into the orientation with the golfing basics of how to rake a sand trap, how to read a putt, how to clean the golfer's clubs and balls etc… But Mr. Olsen was like a broken record and he kept reiterating how important it was how we communicated with the members with both our verbal and nonverbal communication. He was so resolute in making his point of the level of professionalism that was expected.

The caddies in this program would not just caddy for members, but also for their guests and we would also travel to Firestone Country Club and even caddy at PGA Tour events. In summary, Mr. Olsen taught us to be skillful, competent and basically keep our mouth shut and do our job with a good attitude. There is only so much you can learn in a classroom or in this case in an opulent country club stateroom.

Over the next several years I began to learn these principles firsthand out on the course. I climbed up the ranks going all the way from being a "B" caddy to eventually being an "A+" caddy. While out on the golf course I better understood and appreciated Mr. Olsen's instructions on how to talk and when not to talk to the members. The rule of thumb was in most circumstances keep your mouth shut. If the member who we were caddying for or their guest initiated a conversation or comment then and only then was it appropriate to answer them accordingly. But we were there to serve the golfers and not to be too talkative or overstep a boundary. Proverbs 17:28 says it this way, "Even fools are thought wise when they keep silent; with their mouths shut, they seem intelligent."

Ryan Ingram says, "Relational Intelligence is the sum of learned skills that enables us to navigate relationships well." Top business executives and leaders have this common trait, operating with a high level of relational intelligence. Relationships are very delicate. People are sensitive and words are very powerful. Therefore, we need to be alert and careful of what we say, how we say it, and when we say it. What is the most concise way to communicate the message we want to share? What is the best medium to share it through? At what time should we deliver the email, direct message, text message, or phone call? There are so many variables to take into consideration in order to effectively communicate. Having a strong foundation of basic relational intelligence should help to guide us to say the right thing at the right time.

Reflection Question:

How can you improve your relational intelligence?

13

Discover What You
Were Made For

Loving the work you do makes a world of difference and the opposite is also true. Not only does a merry heart or lack thereof towards our work affect our emotions and health but, it also can impact our bottom line. The trait of enjoying what you do is common among those who are crushing it.

On a hot summer day in Georgia after a very satisfying workout, I was relaxing by the pool for a little bit. A gentleman and his wife swimming in the pool were very talkative and started conversing with me. The husband went on and on griping about his job and how he had to go into the graveyard shift later that night. Curious about his job I asked him where he worked? He went on to tell me he was in construction and told me about the big project he was working on on a major Atlanta highway.

I was very intrigued as he told me about all the lack of organization, delays, and problems this highway repair/upgrade job had experienced. The more he talked the more I realized he was unmotivated and despised his job. Now, I worked the overnight shift before when I was getting my start in radio. I understand the difficulty of the sleep schedule and lack thereof when on that shift. But, for this guy, there was a bigger issue than just the sleep depravity. He did not like the work he did. This is nothing against construction, Jesus himself was a carpenter. But, for this fellow, construction was not his forte.

I was recently listening to a message by Shawn Bolz where he described finding a state of flow when we are working where we essentially get lost in the enjoyment of our work that hours and hours pass by and we do not even notice it. The age-old saying is, "Time flies when you are having fun." But, this does not have to only be when you are golfing, fishing, hiking, enjoying some sunshine at the beach, or whatever fun is in your world. This can also be when we are working.

Maybe not every hour of every day, but if we are not doing work that we enjoy, perhaps it's time to rethink the blueprint.

I think about some of my friends like Caleb Auman, Brian Fullerton, and Naylor Taliaferro who I had recently hung out with at a conference in Waco, Texas. They are full of energy, excitement, and passion for their businesses and when I am around them in person I get buoyant and motivated. They love building their businesses and hearing them talk about their work is radically different than the fellow at the pool who was dreading his next shift.

First and foremost let me clarify, the guy with the job he does not like may in fact be a "good guy." I have met his wife and children at the pool as well and I know he sacrifices a lot and works hard to provide for them. I don't want to make it sound like Auman, Fullerton, and Taliaferro are angels and this guy is a demon. But, the stark contrast I do want to draw out is why are some overflowing with ambition and passion about their work, while others seem so apathetic?

The answer may be found in truly finding the work you were called to do. Two resources, other than the Bible, that I have personally found helpful in attempting to discover career purpose is the book *48 days to the Work You Love* by Dan Miller and the podcast *The Ken Coleman Show*. Ken's tagline is Join America's Career Coach, Ken Coleman, as he delivers practical advice to help you discover the role you were born to play—and map out a plan to get you there! As an avid podcast listener, this is a show that has been helpful in my career journey. Ken's new book is *From Paycheck to Purpose* is the clear path to doing work you love. And in addition to Dan Miller's book, he also has many helpful resources available at https://www.48days.com/

With approximately eight billion people on the planet and counting. I clearly do not have the answer for each person as to what job and work are best for your life. Personally, I am still discovering that more and more each day. But, one thing I do believe is that the Lord created us to experience enjoyment and satisfaction in our work. Will it always be a walk in the park? No, but I do believe and strive for finding that work that is life-giving, fulfilling, and produces a good income. This goes well beyond just the pay. But, the overall experience of our work is that we like what we do unlike the fellow at the pool who clearly despised his job, schedule, and in some ways his life.

The tests for me are Sunday evening and Monday morning. I remember as a kid feeling uncomfortable on Sunday evenings. The closer we got to sunset the more the reality set in that it was back to school in the morning. I went to public schools and I did not like it. Now, there are aspects of school that I liked; gym class, recess, lunch, and hanging out with some of my friends. But, many of the other parts of my k-12 experience were burdensome and boring to me. I would watch the clock throughout the day anticipating the next class to end and ultimately to hear that final bell at the end of the school day. I suppose I felt about school how the gentleman at the pool felt about his construction job.

In the late 90s, I enjoyed watching Tiger Woods rise to the top of the golfing world. I was a golfer myself and at that time Tiger was on a roll. He was winning tournaments left and right and I particularly enjoyed watching him play at The Masters Golf Tournament in Augusta, Georgia. Between the beauty of the course, the prestige of the tournament, and Tiger's outright dominance I loved The Masters experience. In those days it seemed to live up to its reputation in the golfing community as a tradition unlike any other. One component of Tiger's game that I appreciated was his concentration and determination throughout the round. He was in it to win it. It was like his opponents feared him. You knew it was going to be an exciting finish if Tiger was in the hunt come Sunday.

But, at that time in the late 90s, for Tiger, the finish was not just on the 18th hole on Sunday. There are stories that after the round, even after a victory, Tiger would head back out to the driving range to fine-tune his game even more. He was obsessed with getting better. Even though he was already ranking as the #1 golfer in the world, his passion would lead him to put in "overtime".

Now, back to my buddy at the pool. He was telling me about his overtime. The project to repair and expand the highway was taking longer than expected and there was some opportunity for overtime pay. But, as he explained it, it was this grudgingly, difficult view of the extra hours. He was motivated by being able to earn some extra money but the pain of having to work longer at a job he hated made him deeply consider if he even wanted to pick up the extra hours to receive the time and a half bonus pay. That was a completely different attitude compared to what Tiger Woods had in the late 90s when he was working "overtime". Tiger on the other hand was fueled by a passion to practice a little longer to tweak his game for peak performance. He was enjoying his work and time was flying by.

Now a caution, please don't close the book, quit your job, and pursue a career on the PGA Tour. Lol, that is not my point. And if you can't break 90, my friend, don't misread what I just wrote. But my point is when we are passionate about the work we do, we can get lost in the long hours, overtime, and full schedules.

As I travel the country and interview business leaders, I find that same passion Tiger had at Augusta National Golf Club in the late 90s, so many of these successful entrepreneurs have it as well. It's beyond the money, they actually enjoy the work they do. They enjoy the process of building what they are building. Just because others may dread their work doesn't mean we have to settle ourselves. Finding whatever it is that we enjoy is a big part of having lasting success. Over the course of our lifetime, we may work around the same amount of time that we sleep so it would be in our best interest to make sure we are doing the work that we were born for.

Recently I was having dinner with a small business owner. He was exploding with excitement when he was telling me what's bubbling in his heart. He had been offered an outrageous amount of money from a large company to buy his business for a large amount. It would be way more than enough for him to retire and enjoy the rest of his life in luxury and with his family. So I asked him if he was considering selling his business. He paused and said maybe because it would free up his time so he could start this new business that he really wanted to do. Retirement wasn't even a thought. His passion for creating and building consumed him. He is already a millionaire and after he sells his business he will be extremely wealthy but it's almost like the money just chases him. He does the work he loves with passion and excellence and the success just seems to follow. Not just monetarily but his marriage is healthy, kids are happy and healthy and his life in many ways is full.

After having dinner with this successful entrepreneur I was fired up. I felt like I was ready to take on the world and take my work to the next level. It was a very different set of emotions that I experienced after eating dinner with this gentleman versus what I felt after talking to the guy at the pool who despised his work.

I'm not saying every person on the planet is destined to be an entre-preneur or small business owner. I do not believe that at all. But, I do believe that we should be diligent in our pursuit of finding work that we actually enjoy doing. The go-getters that I have met, interviewed, and hung out with that are ultra-successful all have that trait in common, they enjoy their work.

I understand that if we don't work, we don't eat. Money does not grow on trees and our bills need to be paid. Not all of us are trust fund babies with a silver spoon. There are real bills to pay and we need to work, earn our pay, and be able to provide for our household. It's okay that for a season we may not be working our dream job but doing what we got to do to make sure ourselves and our loved ones are provided for. But, if that is the case and you are not super excited about your work, then I do believe you should be aggressively praying, studying, and researching in your spare time; asking what work could I do that I enjoy and could earn a good living doing?

Reflection Question

What has God put you on this planet to do?

14

Standing on the
Shoulders of Giants

Building a successful landscaping business involves doing a lot of small things the right way. Since the industry has a relatively low level of entry the market is saturated and profit margins are slimmer compared to many other industries. Throughout this book, I have shared some proven tactics and strategies and in this chapter, I want to summarize what I have learned and believe is the secret recipe for a successful landscaping business.

For starters, counting the cost before building the business is important. There is so much overhead that goes into a landscaping business. Employees, taxes, insurances, equipment, repairs, storage, vehicles, trailers just to name a few. With so many Chuck in the Truck's out there driving the prices down, it takes a lot of attention to detail to achieve lasting profitability. But, with that said, it can be done and as we have discovered in this book it has been done.

As with any business, having the right people on the bus is critical. Many of the problems and stresses landscaping business owners face are around hiring good employees, and when applicable, working with competent, honest sub-contractors. In Chapter 17 of my first book, *Cut That Grass and Make That Cash*, I explained why it pays to work with good subcontractors. Each business leader we referenced in this book has given careful consideration to who they hire. For rookies in the landscaping business, a tendency is to just start growing and figuring it out on the fly. But, there have been countless stories of the business then collapsing when the workload increases but the laborers fail to get the job done on time and the right way, and ultimately the customers are unhappy, and eventually, the finances of the business are struggling. In retrospect, sometimes it's better to build slowly and steadily and ensure you have a good team that can appropriately service your customers.

The next important foundation to a successful, profitable landscaping business is to make sure you are current and stay current with taxes. Based on the data from readers of our first book, we have a diverse international audience and so taxes are obviously different depending on what region of the world you are in. But, the principle of saving money in advance to pay your tax obligations on time is a major key to victory.

As we briefly highlighted in chapter one, the Auman's were able to pay back their mountain of tax debt and today their business is profitable and booming. But, we, unfortunately, have also heard at the Green Industry Podcast countless other stories of those who fell behind on taxes, which eventually destroyed their business and negatively affected other aspects of life.

In order to know how much to set aside for future tax bills, it is recommended to have a trustworthy professional accountant and bookkeeper on your team. The businesses we highlighted throughout this book have the commonality of having their finances organized. Proverbs 27:23 cautions, "Know well the condition of your flocks, and pay attention to your herds." Taking control of your business's finances is essential. My personal bookkeeper, Gulf Coast Bookkeeping, does a great job. In addition to making sure each transaction is properly assigned, once a month we hop on our monthly profit meeting video conference and go over the profit and loss statement, cash flow statement and analyze how the business is truly performing. The numbers tell a story. The more you are intimate with your numbers then the more proactive you can be in making the necessary adjustments to make sure the business is experiencing profitable growth.

When I am not out on the road touring for the Green Industry Podcast I do business consulting, helping landscape business leaders increase profits in their business. Many folks will complain to me that they can't afford to hire a good accountant or bookkeeper, my response is you can't afford not to. Often the solution to pay for the increased expense of hiring an accountant and bookkeeper is to raise the rates for landscaping services.

Knowing your break-even point, budget, and the bottom line is something consultant John Pajak specializes in. In the early days of my landscaping business when I was a rat in the wheel, Pajak spent a good four hours with me going through every expense of my business to help me really get a better picture of what was going on. The conclusion of that "Come to Jesus" meeting was that I needed to raise my prices. I learned that lesson the hard way. The leaders we have spotlighted throughout these pages take charge of their numbers and make sure their services are priced in a way that respects the market yet will ensure the business's profitability. On the other hand, new landscaping businesses often don't truly calculate the true overhead and underprice their services ultimately leading to failure. In a nutshell, the best practice is to know your numbers, charge the right rate to be profitable, and continuously adjust your rates to safeguard your profits. If you need help raising your rates, our ever-popular rate increase letter is available at GreenIndustryPodcast.com - this plug and play template will help you effectively communicate with clients why and how you are raising your prices.

Another best practice we have discussed in this book is that equipment and efficiency are imperative. A noticeable attribute of the business leaders described in this book is that they did not go out and get all the shiny new expensive equipment. Troy Clogg showed me his fleet of hundreds of vehicles. It was impressive to see them lined up row after row. It kind of felt like being at a car dealership as he showed me his fleet. But, Troy reiterated to me that they rarely bought new trucks. They were always shopping for the best deals they could find and many times that meant purchasing a quality used vehicle.

Andy Mulder shared on the Green Industry Podcast his humble beginnings with used equipment. With an eye on profit, it's important to carefully shop for what vehicles, tools, and equipment will get the job done while turning a profit. The business leaders who are winning are in attack mode to find out ways the business can operate with better efficiency. There is often a correlation between efficiency and profits.

Lastly, become an expert at your craft. Quality is an attribute that describes all the leaders referenced in the book. Customers appreciate quality and the job done right. This does not happen by accident. It takes time to develop and train our team members to perform at a high level. When you deliver a quality service at a profitable rate it's a win-win situation. The customer is happy that their outdoor space looks great and our business is happy and healthy when the profits are growing.

Isaac Newton famously quipped, "If I have seen further it is standing on the shoulders of giants." There is a lot we can learn from those who have gone before us. Emulating their best practices while avoiding their mistakes can help us on our journey. Perhaps their ceilings can be our floor as we are launched into our destiny.

At the end of each chapter, there was a reflection question to help assist in furthering to ponder the concept explained in that chapter. My hope and suggestion are that you would prayerfully consider these reflection questions and take the necessary actions to align your life with God's full plan and purposes for you.

What would you like to see changed about your business?

How can you add more value to your customers?

Who has opened doors for you? What doors can you open for others?

What is your plan to improve valuable relationships in your life?

What are your dreams? What are your measurable goals to get from here to there?

What is your plan to improve company culture?

What trends have you noticed lately?
How can your business benefit from these tendencies?

What are you doing to surround yourself
with positive people who challenge you to live a better life?

What can you do in your business to increase efficiency?

What information can you gather to help you make better more informed decisions in the future?

What is one thing you could do better in your business?

How can you improve your people skills?

What are you made for? What is God's destiny for your life?

I hope this book has been a blessing to you. I would like to invite you to stay in touch with us. We have many resources to help you take your business to the next level available at GreenIndustryPodcast. com. Additionally, the Green Industry Podcast is available on all major podcast platforms. We would love for you to join us over in podcast land.

Acknowledgements

I would like to acknowledge my editor who is also my podcast producer, the one and only Mr. Producer. He can be found on Instagram @mrproducerusa and he has been a big blessing to my life. Mr. Producer, thank you for your friendship and all the ways you have made an impact on my podcast and our community. He works with many of the leading podcasts in our industry and if he can be of assistance to you in starting or producing a podcast feel free to send him a DM.